SAINT NICHOLAS

GOD'S GIFT-GIVER

Written and Illustrated by

Hwang Jung-sun

Pauline
BOOKS & MEDIA
Boston

Library of Congress Control Number: 2020933555

CIP data is available.

ISBN 10: 0–8198–9103–7

ISBN 13: 978–0-8198–9103–7

굴뚝으로 들어간 니콜라오 (Nicholas Entered the Chimney)
by HWANG Jung-sun

© 2016 by HWANG Jung-sun, www.pauline.or.kr.

Originally published by Pauline Books & Media, Seoul, Korea.
All rights reserved.

Translated by Unsung Hwang

Copyright © 2021, Daughters of St. Paul for English Edition

Published by Pauline Books & Media, 50 Saint Paul's
Avenue, Boston, MA 02130–3491

Printed in the U.S.A.

SNGGG VSAUSAPEOILL4-1210178 9103-7

www.pauline.org

Pauline Books & Media is the publishing house of the Daughters of
St. Paul, an international congregation of women religious serving
the Church with the communications media.

1 2 3 4 5 6 7 8 9   25 24 23 22 21

CONTENTS

CHAPTER 1

"THERE IS NO SANTA CLAUS!"

3

HOW MANY TIMES HAVE I TOLD YOU TO STOP PLAYING VIDEO GAMES AND GO TO SLEEP?

IF YOU KEEP PLAYING GAMES LIKE THIS, SANTA WON'T BRING YOU ANY PRESENTS THIS YEAR.

SURE.

HE MAY EVEN TAKE AWAY THE PRESENT HE GAVE YOU LAST YEAR.

YOU'RE LYING! THERE IS NO SANTA CLAUS!

THERE IS NO SANTA CLAUS!

YOU THINK I'M STILL A LITTLE KID!

STOMP
STOMP
STOMP
STOMP

4

WHO TOLD YOU THERE'S NO SANTA CLAUS?

HE BROUGHT YOU PRESENTS LAST YEAR!

I SAW HIM COME DOWN THE CHIMNEY WITH THEM.

IF YOU KEEP GOING ON LIKE THIS, SANTA REALLY WON'T BRING YOU ANY GIFTS THIS YEAR!

ONE OF THE FIFTH-GRADE BOYS TOLD ME.

I KNOW YOU AND DAD GAVE ME THOSE PRESENTS LAST CHRISTMAS.

. . . .

SO THERE.

HMPH!

FINE, I WILL TELL YOU THE STORY OF THE **REAL SANTA CLAUS.**

HIS NAME WAS NICHOLAS. HE WAS A SMALL BOY, BUT THE WEALTHIEST IN PATARA! HE HAD EVERYTHING HE WANTED AND COULD DO ANYTHING HE WISHED.

PATARA IN ASIA MINOR, 270 AD

JUST COUNT TO ONE HUNDRED. I WILL GET YOU SOME BREAD BEFORE YOU FINISH.

MOMMY, I'M HUNGRY . . .

HE ALSO TOLD ME TO SELL THESE BRACELETS TO BUY FOOD . . .

IF WE SELL THEM, WE COULD BUY A HOUSE AND OPEN A SMALL STORE!

SO WE AREN'T POOR ANYMORE?

AN ANGEL MUST HAVE COME TO US! THANK YOU, GOD!

11

13

15

16

17

REMEMBER HOW MASTER NICHOLAS FELT LOST AND HEARTBROKEN AFTER HIS PARENTS DIED?

MAYBE AN EVIL SPIRIT ENTERED HIM!

EVIL SPIRIT, GO AWAY!

NO WAY! HOW COULD SUCH A THING HAPPEN TO HIM?

WE'VE TRIED SO HARD TO PROTECT HIM FROM EVERYTHING . . .

AS I WAS SAYING: HE FELT EMPTY AFTER HIS PARENTS DIED . . .

. . . THEN AN EVIL SPIRIT POSSESSED HIM.

AFTER ALL, EVIL USUALLY WAITS UNTIL THE HEART IS WEAKEST.

21

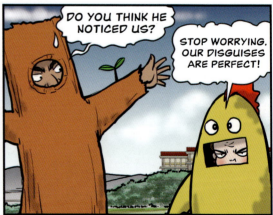

HE'S STEALING!

HE JUST STOLE SOMETHING FROM THAT FOOD BASKET! HE'S RUNNING AWAY!

DASH!
푸다닥

WHAT DID HE STEAL?

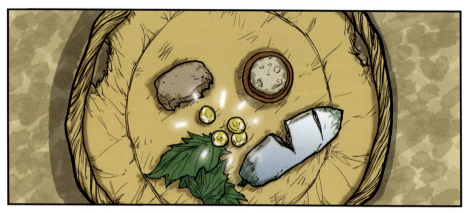

ARE THOSE GOLD COINS?

GOLD COINS AND MOLDY BREAD?

DO YOU THINK THE YOUNG MASTER—

THWACK!

WHAT?! WHO THREW THAT?!

PLUNK!

GET OUT OF HERE!

LEAVE US ALONE, STRANGE MONSTERS!

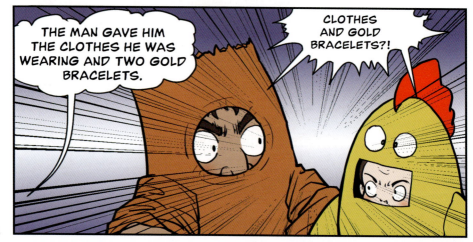

IF YOU LEAD US TO YOUR NEIGHBOR'S HOUSE, WE'LL LET YOU KEEP THESE GOLD COINS.

REALLY? LET'S GO NOW!

FIRST, LET'S GET OUT OF THESE COSTUMES.

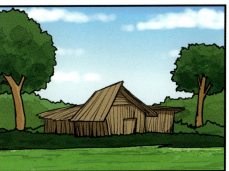

THESE BRACELETS ARE . . . !

SO IT'S TRUE!

WE'LL BUY THESE BRACELETS FROM YOU! WE'LL GIVE YOU GOOD MONEY FOR THEM.

THAT'S NOT NECESSARY! THEY'RE NOT MINE TO SELL.

EVEN SO, THE YOUNG MAN GAVE THEM TO YOU FOR A REASON. HERE, TAKE THE MONEY.

THIS IS SO MUCH . . . THANK YOU.

NICHOLAS' VILLA

29

THESE GOLD BRACELETS . . .

WITH THESE . . .

... THAT MOTHER AND HER CHILD COULD HAVE ENJOYED MANY HOT MEALS TOGETHER.

WHY DID YOU TAKE AWAY THEIR CHANCE FOR SOME COMFORT?

DON'T WORRY. I GAVE THEM ENOUGH MONEY TO OPEN A SMALL RESTAURANT.

WHY ARE YOU PLAYING THIS GAME?

YOU THINK IT'S A GAME?

THE TRUTH IS ... I'M NOT HAPPY.

MOM! DAD!

I'M OVER HERE!

M-MOM...?
D-DAD...?

35

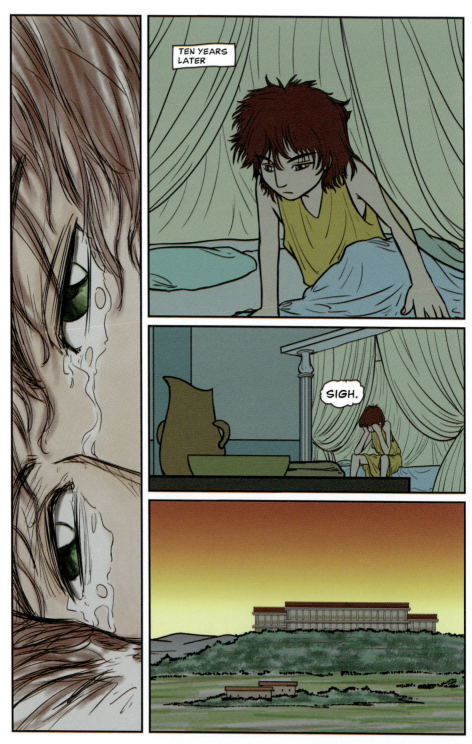

YOUR PHILOSOPHY AND GREEK TUTOR IS COMING THIS MORNING. HE WILL BE STAYING HERE FOR THE NEXT SIX MONTHS, SO PLEASE TREAT HIM RESPECTFULLY.

AND IN THE AFTERNOON . . .

THOSE PUPPY EYES WON'T CHANGE A THING . . .

NANNY, YOU LOOK ESPECIALLY PRETTY TODAY.

YOU WON'T GET OUT OF YOUR LESSONS THAT WAY!

SURELY THE LESSONS CAN WAIT . . .

NICHOLAS!

COME BACK! DO YOU KNOW HOW HARD IT WAS TO BRING YOUR TUTOR HERE? UGH . . .

CATCH HIM! DON'T LET HIM ESCAPE!

SORRY, NANNY. BUT I REALLY DON'T FEEL LIKE STUDYING TODAY.

YOUNG MASTER!

WHERE IS HE?

WHAM!

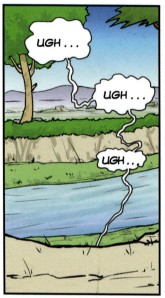

UGH...

UGH...

UGH...

WHAT ARE YOU DOING?

YOGA?

WHY ARE YOU JUST WATCHING ME? HELP ME UP!

CRUNCH! CRACK!

CAREFUL! EASY!

I MUST BE REALLY SICK... I WAS JUST GOING TO THE STREAM FOR SOME WATER...

... WHEN THE SKY TURNED YELLOW AND I PASSED OUT.

GROWL

GRUMBLE

HOW MUCH LONGER MUST I SUFFER? CAN THIS REALLY BE GOD'S WILL?

GRUMBLE

GOD'S WILL . . . A WILL! I MUST WRITE MY WILL!

GROWL

GRUMBLE

WHEN WAS THE LAST TIME YOU ATE?

THREE DAYS? OR MAYBE FIVE . . .

GROWL

GRUMBLE

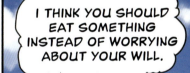

I THINK YOU SHOULD EAT SOMETHING INSTEAD OF WORRYING ABOUT YOUR WILL.

YOU MAY BE RIGHT. COME TO THINK OF IT, I **AM** REALLY HUNGRY.

HOW FAR AWAY IS THE CLOSEST RESTAURANT?

GROWL

JUST A LITTLE FURTHER!

OH! THE SKY IS TURNING YELLOW AGAIN . . .

I'LL CARRY YOU!

YOU SURE?

IT'S SOOOO GOOD!

HOW CAN FOOD BE SO DELICIOUS?

WELL, IT **HAS** BEEN DAYS SINCE YOU'VE EATEN.

IT TASTES HEAVENLY!

벌컥
GULP

벌컥
CHOMP

TEACHER!

TEACHER, WHEN DID YOU ARRIVE? WE'VE BEEN WAITING FOR YOU!

I JUST GOT HERE.

41

DON'T WORRY, WE PAID THE BILL—

OH, I SHOULD REWARD YOU FOR HELPING OUR PRIEST...

NO, PLEASE HELP ME.

COME, BROTHER!

LET US GO TOGETHER.

THE CHURCH OF PATARA

THIS IS THE BOOK OF LIFE.

IN IT, YOU WILL FIND THE WORDS OF JESUS—AND YOU WILL MEET JESUS IN HIS WORD.

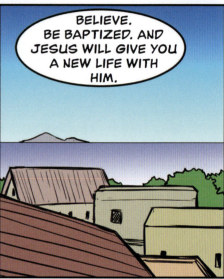

BELIEVE. BE BAPTIZED. AND JESUS WILL GIVE YOU A NEW LIFE WITH HIM.

I SAW IT! I SAW IT!

BAM!

49

NICHOLAS IN LOVE? COULD IT BE?

IT'S TRUE THAT HE'S NOT A CHILD ANYMORE.

I WONDER WHAT KIND OF GIRL SHE IS . . .

AND IT IS NICE SEEING HIS BRIGHT, HAPPY FACE AGAIN—LIKE WHEN HE WAS YOUNGER.

TSK TSK, HE LEFT HIS LIGHT ON AGAIN . . .

51

WHAT ARE YOU DOING?

I AM READING JESUS' WORDS.

OH . . . I SEE.

JESUS . . .

SIGH

I FAILED. I TRIED SO HARD TO MAKE MASTER NICHOLAS SMILE . . . I TRIED FOR YEARS . . . BUT ONLY JESUS SUCCEEDED.

JESUS?

YES! FIND THIS GIRL NAMED "JESUS" IMMEDIATELY! MASTER NICHOLAS STAYED UP ALL NIGHT READING HER LOVE LETTER. I NEED TO KNOW WHO SHE IS AND WHERE SHE LIVES!

I NEED TO KNOW HOW PRETTY SHE IS, TOO, TO MAKE THE YOUNG MASTER SMILE LIKE THAT.

WHAT IS IT ABOUT HER?

HE'S NEVER BEEN IN LOVE BEFORE.

THIS IS A NEW SIDE OF HIM!

MASTER NICHOLAS ROCKS!

CHAPTER 2

LEAVING ALL FOR CHRIST

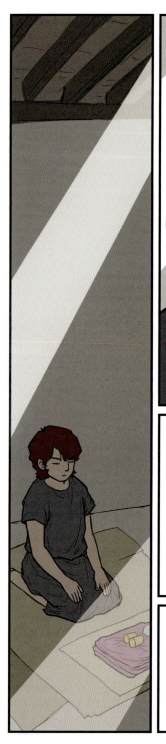

I DO BELIEVE. JESUS HAS THE WORDS OF EVERLASTING LIFE. HE IS THE WORD OF LIFE . . .

. . . AND MY BAPTISM HAS MADE ME ONE WITH HIM.

IN JESUS, I HAVE EVERYTHING I NEED.

I AM READY TO START A NEW LIFE WITH HIM. I'VE GIVEN AWAY EVERYTHING I HAVE . . .

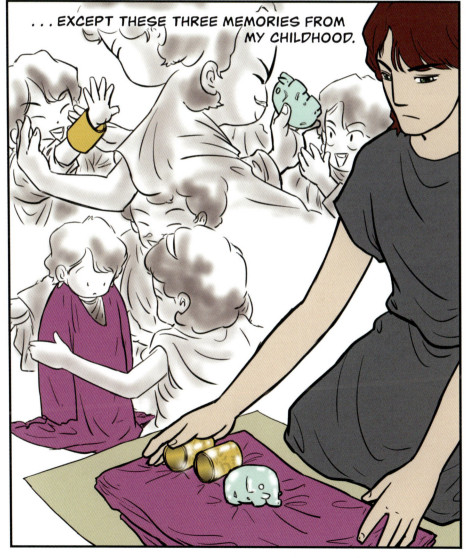

. . . EXCEPT THESE THREE MEMORIES FROM MY CHILDHOOD.

SHOULD I KEEP THESE WITH ME?

I HEARD THEY'RE SELLING ALL THREE OF THEIR DAUGHTERS.

ISN'T THE ELDEST GETTING MARRIED?

HER FAMILY DOESN'T HAVE MONEY FOR THE WEDDING.

I HEARD THE MOTHER HAS A SERIOUS ILLNESS.

YES, SHE SPENT ALL HER MONEY ON MEDICAL TREATMENTS...

NOW SHE HAS A HUGE DEBT TO PAY OFF. THAT'S WHY SHE HAS TO SELL HER DAUGHTERS.

59

THIS IS WHY I TOLD MASTER NICHOLAS THAT WE NEED A STATUE OF HIM BY THE WELL . . .

HE'S DONATED EVERYTHING TO THIS TOWN. HE EVEN DIVIDED ALL HIS BELONGINGS BETWEEN US, HIS SERVANTS, AND SET US FREE. NOW WHO WILL TAKE CARE OF HIM?

YOU SHOULD SHOW THE YOUNG MASTER MORE RESPECT!

HUH?

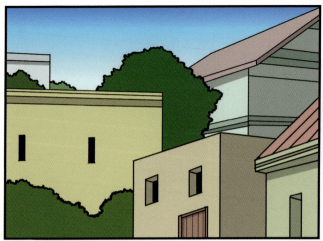
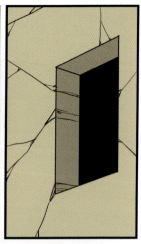

THESE BRACELETS SHOULD BE ENOUGH TO CANCEL THEIR DEBT AND PAY FOR THE ELDEST DAUGHTER'S WEDDING.

HMM . . . I CAN SELL ONE ITEM AT A TIME . . .

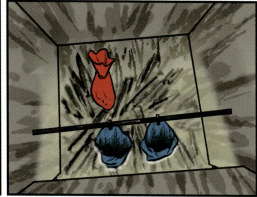

WITH THAT MONEY, THEY CAN TAKE CARE OF THEIR DEBT AND PAY FOR THE WEDDING.

AS SOON AS THE SUN RISES, I'M GOING TO SELL MY PURPLE ROBE . . .

THE NEXT NIGHT

THUNK!

I TOSSED THAT MONEY INTO THE SACK EVEN BETTER THAN LAST NIGHT! I'M GETTING GOOD!

NOW, TO SELL MY ELEPHANT STATUE . . .

THE NEXT NIGHT

살금
TIPTOE

살금
TIPTOE

THIS PLACE IS STARTING TO FEEL LIKE HOME, NOW THAT I'VE COME HERE SO OFTEN.

AND NOW, FOR THE LAST GIFT.

THIS MONEY IS FOR THE YOUNGEST DAUGHTER. IT SHOULD BUY HER ALL THE FOOD SHE WANTS, PLUS PAY FOR HER WEDDING SOMEDAY.

HEY, WHERE ARE THE SACKS?

OH!

HERE.

FOR THE YOUNGEST DAUGHTER.

MY LORD AND MASTER IS JESUS CHRIST, THE SON OF GOD. HE CAME INTO THE WORLD TO FREE US FROM SIN AND MAKE US CHILDREN OF GOD THE FATHER.

HUH?

BY THE WAY . . . WHY DID YOU HAVE SACKS HANGING IN YOUR CHIMNEY? DID YOU KNOW I WAS COMING?

WHAT? SACKS?

OH, THESE AREN'T SACKS. THEY'RE SOCKS THAT I HUNG UP TO DRY.

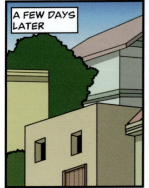

A FEW DAYS LATER

LORD, NOW I HAVE TRULY GIVEN UP EVERYTHING. I AM READY TO FOLLOW YOU WITH ALL MY HEART.

I WILL TAKE THE LOWEST PLACE. I WILL BECOME A PRIEST, A SERVANT OF YOUR CHURCH.

I WILL GIVE YOU ALL OF MYSELF.

A FEW YEARS LATER

FATHER, ARE YOU LEAVING ALREADY?

YES. I HAD HOPED TO SPEND THE REST OF MY LIFE SERVING GOD'S PEOPLE IN PATARA . . .

. . . BUT I FEEL THE LORD URGING ME TO GO TO MYRA. WHEN I GET THERE, I TRUST THAT HE WILL SHOW ME WHAT I MUST DO.

I HEARD YOU'RE GOING TO MYRA, SO I PACKED YOU A LITTLE FOOD.

A LITTLE . . . ?

YOU MUST EAT THIS FISH BY TONIGHT, OR IT WILL GO BAD. THIS BREAD GOES WITH THIS CHEESE, AND YOU'LL NEED TO ROAST THIS CHICKEN OVER A CAMPFIRE BEFORE YOU EAT IT.

I CAN'T TAKE THIS WAGON WITH ME. I HAVE TO WALK THROUGH THE MOUNTAINS!

THEN I WILL COME WITH AND PULL THE WAGON FOR YOU.

NO! I WILL CARRY IT MYSELF!

I KNOW HE IS DOING GOD'S WILL, BUT IT STILL BREAKS MY HEART TO SEE HIM WEARING THOSE RAGS . . .

SNIFF

I CAN DO THIS!

I CAN DO THIS!

부들

부들

WOBBLE

WOBBLE

THE CHURCH OF MYRA

WHAT ARE WE GOING TO DO? MYRA NEEDS A NEW BISHOP, BUT EACH OF US WANTS TO ELECT A DIFFERENT PERSON TO FILL THIS ROLE. WHAT IF WE CAN'T AGREE?

LET'S DRAW NAMES!

LET'S PLAY ROCK-PAPER-SCISSORS!

WATCH ME WIN!

LET'S CHOOSE THE OLDEST . . .

WHOEVER IS LEFT-HANDED!

NONSENSE!

I CAN USE BOTH HANDS!

ENOUGH!

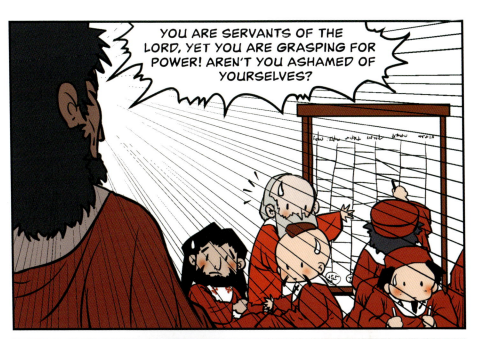

. . . SHALL BE THE NEXT BISHOP OF MYRA.

THE NEXT MORNING

THAT FISH SURE WAS TASTY . . . NOW THAT I'VE ARRIVED IN MYRA, I SHOULD FIND A CHURCH AND PRAY.

85

WHAT?
A CHURCH FULL OF
PRIESTS, THIS EARLY
IN THE MORNING?
SOMETHING'S
GOING ON!

SHOULD I BACK OUT
AND CLOSE THE DOOR?
OR . . .

LEAP!
LEAP!

AH!

I SHOULDN'T HAVE DONE THAT. I SHOULD HAVE LEFT . . .

I FEEL LIKE I'M INTERRUPTING SOMETHING VERY IMPORTANT.

THE FIRST ONE TO STEP IN!

THE FIRST ONE TO STEP IN!

WHO ARE YOU?

IT'S THAT PRIEST FROM PATARA!

FATHER NICHOLAS!

GOOD MORNING.

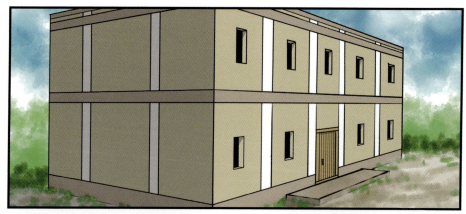

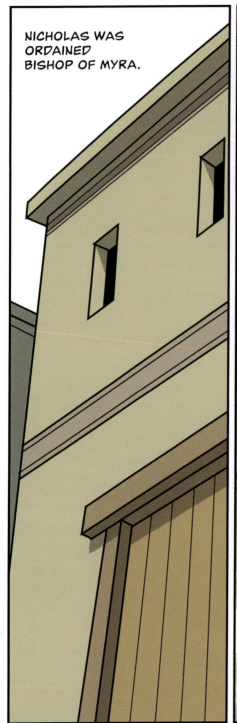

NICHOLAS WAS ORDAINED BISHOP OF MYRA.

AND WITHIN THE NEXT YEAR, THE WEIGHT OF HIS RESPONSIBILITY INCREASED.

CHAPTER 3

TRIALS AND FAITH

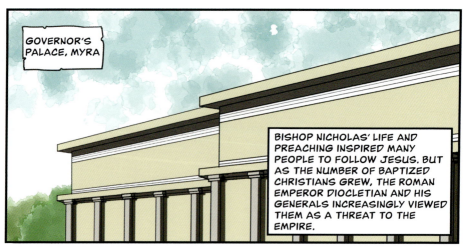

GOVERNOR'S PALACE, MYRA

BISHOP NICHOLAS' LIFE AND PREACHING INSPIRED MANY PEOPLE TO FOLLOW JESUS. BUT AS THE NUMBER OF BAPTIZED CHRISTIANS GREW, THE ROMAN EMPEROR DIOCLETIAN AND HIS GENERALS INCREASINGLY VIEWED THEM AS A THREAT TO THE EMPIRE.

I'M SO BORED THESE DAYS. SOMETIMES I EVEN MISS HAVING GENERAL GAIUS AROUND.

GAIUS?! IT'S ONLY BEEN TWO YEARS SINCE THAT PSYCHO GENERAL WENT TO ROME! HE WORKED US SO HARD BACK THEN, I WAS LITTLE MORE THAN A BAG OF BONES . . .

GENERAL GAIUS HAS ARRIVED FROM ROME!

WHAT?! WHY IS HE BACK SO SUDDENLY?

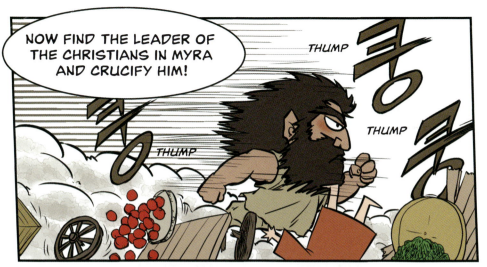

98

I'VE JUST BEEN INFORMED . . .

. . . THAT ROMAN SOLDIERS ARE ON THEIR WAY TO CAPTURE AND CRUCIFY YOU!

SO HURRY!

I AM . . .

. . . THE BISHOP OF MYRA.

THIS POSITION WAS GIVEN TO ME BY GOD. IT IS NOT SOMETHING I CAN RUN AWAY FROM.

HE COULD MESMERIZE ALL OF MYRA IN LESS THAN A YEAR.

LOOK. ALL YOU NEED TO DO IS DENY THAT JESUS IS GOD AND WORSHIP THE ROMAN GODS IN OUR TEMPLE.

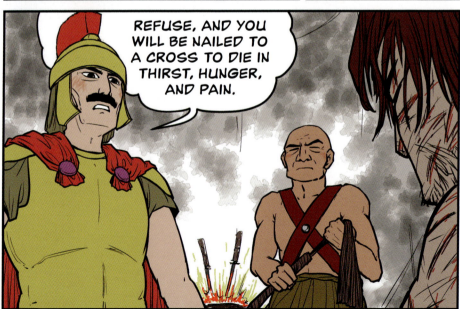

REFUSE, AND YOU WILL BE NAILED TO A CROSS TO DIE IN THIRST, HUNGER, AND PAIN.

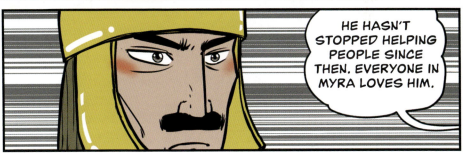

AND SO
NICHOLAS

WAS IMPRISONED, NOT
KNOWING IF OR WHEN HE
WOULD BE RELEASED.

MANY CHRISTIANS, INCLUDING BISHOPS AND PRIESTS, WERE IMPRISONED, TORTURED, AND KILLED DURING THE REIGN OF THE ROMAN EMPEROR DIOCLETIAN.

THIS GREAT PERSECUTION (303–313 AD) WAS THE LAST, AND WORST, PERSECUTION OF CHRISTIANS IN THE ROMAN EMPIRE.

IN 313 AD, THE ROMAN EMPERORS CONSTANTINE AND LICINIUS TOGETHER ISSUED THE EDICT OF MILAN. THIS GAVE LEGAL STATUS TO CHRISTIANITY IN THE ROMAN EMPIRE. CHRISTIANS WERE NOW FREE TO PRACTICE THEIR FAITH.

THE EMPERORS PLEDGED TO RETURN ALL THE MONEY AND PROPERTY THEY HAD TAKEN FROM THE CHURCH DURING THE PERSECUTION.

THE EDICT ALSO FREED THOSE CHRISTIANS WHO HAD BEEN IMPRISONED FOR THEIR FAITH—INCLUDING NICHOLAS.

'CONGRATS!'

경 주교님석방 축

BISHOP

ISN'T BISHOP NICHOLAS BEING RELEASED THIS AFTERNOON?

ISN'T IT TODAY?

THEY DEFINITELY SAID THE YOUNG MASTER WOULD BE RELEASED TODAY.

THEY SHOULD'VE RELEASED THE BISHOP FIRST!

UM . . . I AM NICHOL—

AH!

THREE HOURS LATER

NICHOLAS FINALLY PERSUADED EVERYONE THAT HE WAS, INDEED, NICHOLAS.

BISHOP NICHOLAS, I MISSED YOU!

OH, YOUNG MASTER! YOU MUST HAVE SUFFERED SO MUCH! LOOK AT YOUR FACE!

HOORAY, BISHOP NICHOLAS!

BUT THERE WERE STILL A FEW SKEPTICS WHO NEVER BELIEVED HIM.

WHEN NICHOLAS LOOKED IN A MIRROR FOR THE
FIRST TIME AFTER HIS RELEASE, HE ALMOST
DIDN'T BELIEVE HIMSELF, EITHER.

CHAPTER 4

SIGNS AND WONDERS

SUNDAY	MONDAY	TUESDAY	WEDNESDAY	THURSDAY	FRIDAY	SATURDAY

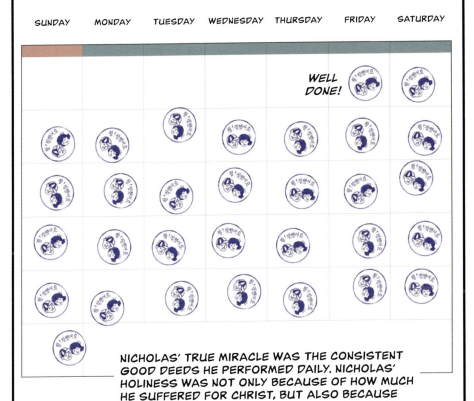

WELL DONE!

NICHOLAS' TRUE MIRACLE WAS THE CONSISTENT GOOD DEEDS HE PERFORMED DAILY. NICHOLAS' HOLINESS WAS NOT ONLY BECAUSE OF HOW MUCH HE SUFFERED FOR CHRIST, BUT ALSO BECAUSE OF THE MANY ACTS OF LOVE HE PERFORMED IN CHRIST'S NAME EVERY DAY.

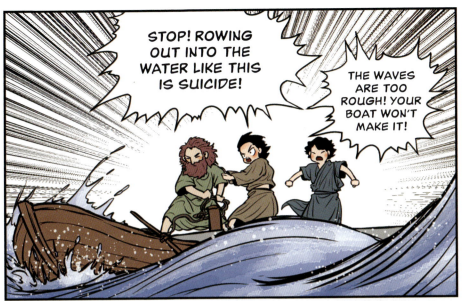

121

KEEP YOUR
HEAD UP!

GRAB THE
ROPE!
YES, LIKE
THAT!

BUILD MORE FIRES! GIVE THEM WATER AND FOOD!

FIND SOME DRY CLOTHES!

?

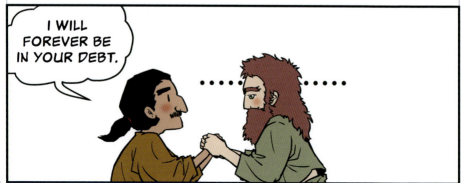

126

NICHOLAS CONTINUED PERFORMING MANY OTHER GOOD DEEDS—ALL FOR THE SAKE OF LIVING AND PREACHING THE GOSPEL OF JESUS CHRIST.

PEOPLE WERE HUNGRY FOR THIS TRUTH. AT THAT TIME, SEVERAL HERESIES—FALSE TEACHINGS—WERE CONFUSING CHRISTIANS AND LEADING THEM ASTRAY.

WHEN THE ROMAN EMPEROR CONSTANTINE HEARD ABOUT THIS, HE CALLED ALL THE BISHOPS IN THE EMPIRE TO A SPECIAL MEETING, OR COUNCIL, SO THEY COULD CLARIFY THE TEACHINGS OF THE CHURCH.

COUNCIL OF NICAEA, 325 AD

I, ARIUS, HAVE SPOKEN! JESUS IS NOT GOD; HE IS ONLY THE GREATEST CREATURE MADE BY GOD. THERE IS NO SUCH THING AS THE HOLY TRINITY!

ONLY . . . HUH?

THUMP THUMP THUMP

다 다 다다

129

131

*AN OMOPHORION IS A VESTMENT WORN BY BISHOPS IN THE EASTERN CATHOLIC CHURCH. IT IS A SIGN OF THE BISHOP'S AUTHORITY AS LEADER AND SHEPHERD OF HIS PEOPLE.

LORD!

THE NEXT MORNING

BISHOP NICHOLAS, ARE YOU AWAKE? IT'S TIME FOR BREAKFAST . . .

I WAS ON GUARD ALL NIGHT! WHERE DID HE GET THAT BOOK AND GARMENT? NO WAY!

THIS IS A MIRACLE! A MIRACLE HAPPENED—RIGHT HERE!

AS NEWS OF THE MIRACLE SPREAD, MANY PEOPLE FLOCKED TO NICHOLAS' CELL TO SEE FOR THEMSELVES WHAT HAD HAPPENED.

ALL WERE ASTONISHED AND GAVE GLORY AND PRAISE TO GOD. EMPEROR CONSTANTINE IMMEDIATELY ORDERED THAT NICHOLAS BE SET FREE.

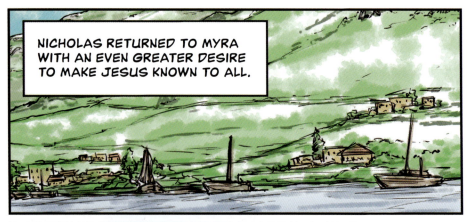

NICHOLAS RETURNED TO MYRA WITH AN EVEN GREATER DESIRE TO MAKE JESUS KNOWN TO ALL.

GOVERNOR'S PALACE, MYRA

BANG!

오당탕

GENERAL GAIUS! WHY DIDN'T YOU TELL US YOU WERE COMING IN FROM ROME? WE WOULD HAVE BEEN HERE TO GREET YOU!

WE WERE OUT IN THE FIELDS. THERE'S A TERRIBLE DROUGHT . . .

141

143

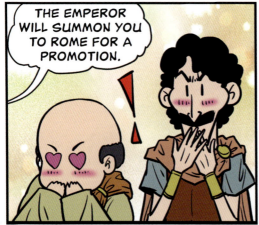

MANY STARVING PEOPLE LEFT MYRA FOR THE "DREAM JOB" IN THE MINES.

ONE YEAR LATER

HEY, WHAT'S THAT?

A BEGGAR.

DEAR, LET'S GIVE THE MAN SOME BREAD AND SEND HIM ON HIS WAY.

WAIT, YOUR GAME PIECE WASN'T ON THIS SQUARE!

WHAT ARE YOU TALKING ABOUT?

AAAH!

HEY!

LEAVE MY WIFE ALONE, YOU BEGGAR!

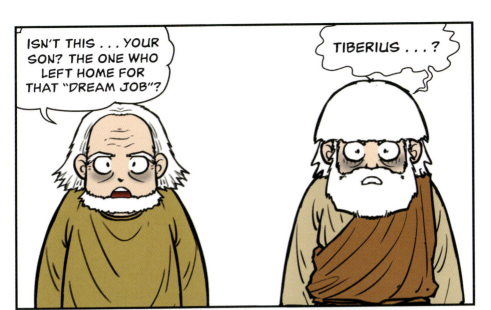

HE WAS A DEVIL.

OH MY, YOUR HAND MUST REALLY HURT FROM THAT INJURY.

IT WAS CRUSHED BY A FALLING ROCK. WHAT SHOULD WE DO WITH HIM?

POOR THING.

WELL, HE WON'T GROW A NEW HAND. KILL HIM AND THROW AWAY THE BODY.

AH . . .

I AM TRYING VERY HARD TO FIND THE PEOPLE WHO WERE SOLD.

NO! MY DADDY'S IN THIS PICTURE!

꿈의 일자리!
DREAM JOB!

DON'T STARVE DURING THE DROUGHT! WORK FOR ONE YEAR AND EARN ENOUGH TO BUY A FARM! APPLY TODAY!

OH. I'M AFRAID I CAN'T DO MUCH ABOUT THAT. HE'S IN PRISON BECAUSE HE COMMITTED A GRAVE CRIME . . .

NO!

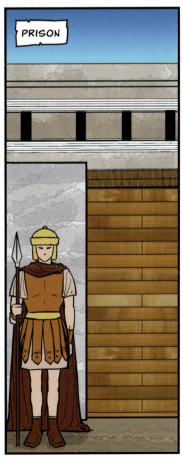

VERY WELL. TELL ME IN DETAIL WHAT HAPPENED.

IT ALL STARTED A YEAR AGO. AS YOU KNOW, PEOPLE WERE SUFFERING FROM THE DROUGHT.

GENERAL GAIUS SHOWED UP IN MYRA WITH A MAN WHO OWNED A GOLD MINE . . .

NICHOLAS MET WITH EVERY OFFICIAL IN THE PRISON. HE SOON LEARNED THE TRUTH ABOUT MYRA'S ENSLAVEMENT.

159

EMPEROR CONSTANTINE?

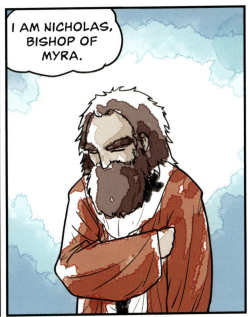

CONSTANTINE'S PALACE, ROME

PANT

PANT

PANT

RING RING

THE LORD SPOKE TO ME IN MY DREAM.

MASTER, DID YOU CALL?

FETCH MY CHIEF INSPECTOR AT ONCE!

THE NEXT MORNING, GENERAL GAIUS' VILLA, ROME

HOW DARE YOU? DO YOU KNOW WHO I AM? I AM GENERAL GAIUS! IF YOU DO NOT LEAVE AT ONCE . . .

THIS IS THE ORDER OF EMPEROR CONSTANTINE!

ARREST GENERAL GAIUS AND SEIZE HIS PROPERTY AND POSSESSIONS!

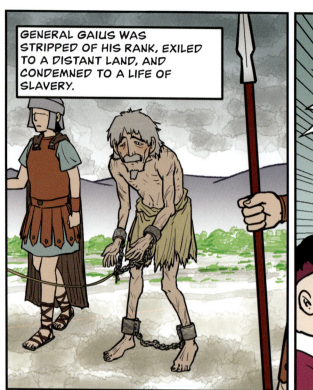

GENERAL GAIUS WAS STRIPPED OF HIS RANK, EXILED TO A DISTANT LAND, AND CONDEMNED TO A LIFE OF SLAVERY.

MY LORD! ROMAN SOLDIERS HAVE ARRIVED!

GIVE THEM SOME MONEY AND SEND THEM AWAY.

I DON'T THINK THAT'S POSSIBLE.

THERE'S AN ARMY OF THEM. WE'RE COMPLETELY SURROUNDED!

THE SLAVE MERCHANT WAS ARRESTED AND PUNISHED FOR HIS CRIME.

THE PEOPLE OF MYRA WERE FINALLY FREE. WHEN THEY RETURNED HOME, CONSTANTINE DISTRIBUTED THE RICHES OF GENERAL GAIUS AND THE SLAVE MERCHANT AMONG THEM.

DADDY?

DADDY!

THE EMPEROR ALSO FREED THE OFFICIALS HE HAD WRONGFULLY IMPRISONED.

DISGRACED EX-GENERAL
"REGRETS" HIS ACTIONS

CHAPTER 5

NICHOLAS THE SAINT

MANY YEARS LATER, MYRA WAS STRUCK BY ANOTHER SEVERE DROUGHT.

HELP!

I SAID, "HELP" . . .

HELP?! WHAT HAPPENED?

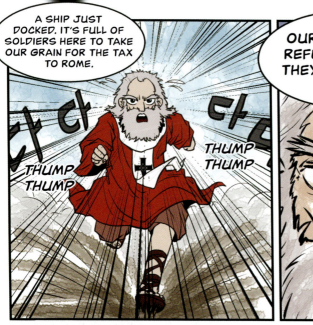

170

THIS GRAIN IS ALL WE HAVE!

ROME IS OVERFLOWING WITH FOOD!

OUR CHILDREN ARE STARVING!

YOU OWE THIS TAX TO THE EMPEROR!

NOW GIVE US YOUR GRAIN OR PREPARE TO DIE!

CAPTAIN'S CABIN

I CAN'T! IF I LOSE ANY GRAIN FROM THIS SHIP, THE EMPEROR WILL KILL ME.

AND IF YOU DON'T SHARE THE GRAIN YOU HAVE ONBOARD, COUNTLESS PEOPLE WILL STARVE!

I'VE ONLY COLLECTED GRAIN FROM A FEW REGIONS. IT'S NOT ENOUGH TO FEED EVERYONE.

WE JUST NEED TWO MONTHS' WORTH OF GRAIN. BY THEN, THE BARLEY WILL BE GROWING AGAIN. IF YOU WAIVE OUR TAX AND SHARE SOME OF WHAT YOU HAVE, OUR PEOPLE WILL LIVE.

BUT I AM RESPONSIBLE FOR GETTING THIS GRAIN SAFELY TO ROME.

AND JUST HOW DO YOU PLAN TO DO THAT? LOOK AT WHAT'S HAPPENING OUTSIDE. DO YOU WANT TO SEE BLOODSHED?

OF COURSE NOT. THAT'S WHY YOU MUST CONVINCE THE CROWD TO BACK OFF.

HOW CAN ANYONE . . .

BISHOP NICHOLAS, ARE YOU ALRIGHT?

. . . CONVINCE THEM . . .

. . . WAIT! DO I KNOW YOU?

NO, YOU DON'T!

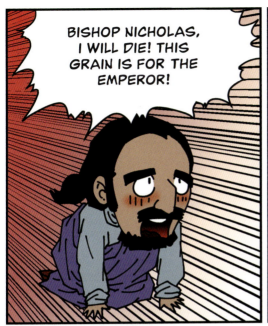

HUH? WHAT DO YOU MEAN?

THOSE PEOPLE OUTSIDE RISKED THEIR LIVES TO SAVE YOU AND YOUR CREW WHEN YOUR SHIP WAS DASHED TO PIECES.

NOW THEY ARE DYING OF HUNGER. ALL I ASK IS THAT YOU SHARE A LITTLE FOOD WITH THEM.

ALRIGHT. I WILL SHARE MY GRAIN. BUT BISHOP NICHOLAS . . . PLEASE PRAY FOR ME.

THE LORD WILL REFILL YOUR GRAIN. DO NOT WORRY.

THE CAPTAIN UNLOADED THE GRAIN AND DISTRIBUTED IT TO THE PEOPLE OF MYRA.

OSTIA, PORT CITY OF ROME

I'M AN IDIOT! AN IDIOT! NOW ONLY DEATH AWAITS ME.

CAPTAIN'S CABIN

UNLESS I TELL THEM BISHOP NICHOLAS FORCED ME TO DO IT. PERHAPS THEY WON'T KILL ME THEN.

CREAK

TREMBLE

GASP

181

"GOOD QUALITY?"

"SAFELY?"

"ALL?"

HUFF

HUFF

HUFF

HUFF

ALL THE GRAIN IS HERE! ALL OF IT!

O LORD, THANK YOU! YOU SAVED ME!

GIVE ME YOUR SIGNATURE! SIGN!

ALLELUIA!

NICHOLAS' LIFE OF PRAYER AND SERVICE BROUGHT HOPE TO THE PEOPLE OF MYRA—ESPECIALLY THOSE SUFFERING FROM INJUSTICE.

WE ARE ON DEATH ROW.

AND WE ARE ALL IN OUR TWENTIES.

REALLY.

185

187

BISHOP NICHOLAS CLEARED THE MEN'S NAMES AND WON THEIR FREEDOM.

SO NOW, WE ARE FREE MEN.

WE ALSO LOOK YOUNG AGAIN. EXCEPT FOR ONE OF US ...

DID I USE THE WRONG FACE CREAM?

THE REAL MURDERERS WERE ARRESTED AND PUNISHED, ALONG WITH THE EVIL INVESTIGATORS. BUT WE STILL HAD ONE MORE OBSTACLE TO FACE ...

BISHOP NICHOLAS!

PLEASE FIND US A JOB.

IS MY FACE STUCK LIKE THIS?

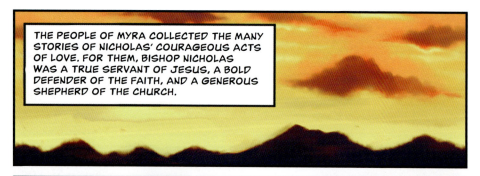

THE PEOPLE OF MYRA COLLECTED THE MANY STORIES OF NICHOLAS' COURAGEOUS ACTS OF LOVE. FOR THEM, BISHOP NICHOLAS WAS A TRUE SERVANT OF JESUS, A BOLD DEFENDER OF THE FAITH, AND A GENEROUS SHEPHERD OF THE CHURCH.

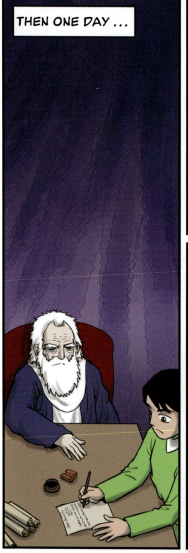

THEN ONE DAY ...

I'M A LITTLE TIRED. I'D BETTER REST.

I'LL WALK YOU TO YOUR BEDROOM.

NO, I'LL JUST REST IN THIS CHAIR FOR A LITTLE BIT.

ALRIGHT. IF YOU NEED ANYTHING, CALL FOR ME.

ON DECEMBER 6, 343, NICHOLAS FELL ASLEEP IN THE ARMS OF THE LORD.

WHEN A SAINT LEAVES THIS WORLD FOR HEAVEN, HE PRAYS FOR US SO THAT WE MAY BE INSPIRED TO DO EVEN GREATER ACTS OF FAITH, HOPE, AND LOVE.

THE STORIES OF SAINT NICHOLAS' GENEROSITY AND COURAGE SPREAD THROUGHOUT EUROPE.

NICHOLAS BECAME A PATRON SAINT OF CHILDREN AND SAILORS, WHOM HE HAD PROTECTED DURING HIS LIFE.

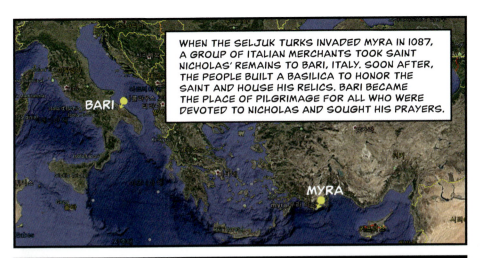

WHEN THE SELJUK TURKS INVADED MYRA IN 1087, A GROUP OF ITALIAN MERCHANTS TOOK SAINT NICHOLAS' REMAINS TO BARI, ITALY. SOON AFTER, THE PEOPLE BUILT A BASILICA TO HONOR THE SAINT AND HOUSE HIS RELICS. BARI BECAME THE PLACE OF PILGRIMAGE FOR ALL WHO WERE DEVOTED TO NICHOLAS AND SOUGHT HIS PRAYERS.

IN THE EARLY TWELFTH CENTURY, PEOPLE IN FRANCE AND BELGIUM BEGAN THE CUSTOM OF GIVING GIFTS TO POOR CHILDREN ON DECEMBER 5, THE DAY BEFORE SAINT NICHOLAS' FEAST DAY.

THEY TOLD THE CHILDREN THAT IF THEY PUT OUT THEIR SOCKS OR SHOES, SAINT NICHOLAS WOULD COME DOWN THE CHIMNEY AND FILL THEM WITH GIFTS.

IN FOURTH-CENTURY MYRA, NICHOLAS WAS KNOWN AS "NIKOLAOS," THE GREEK VERSION OF NICHOLAS. IN LATIN, THE LANGUAGE OF THE CHURCH, HE BECAME "SANCTUS NICOLAUS" (SAINT NICHOLAS). TO THE DUTCH, HE BECAME "SINTERKLAAS."

SANCTUS NICOLAUS!

SINTERKLAAS!

OVER TIME, ENGLISH-SPEAKERS CHANGED THE PRONUNCIATION OF "SINTERKLAAS" TO "SANTA CLAUS," AS WE KNOW IT TODAY.

SINTERKLAAS!

SANTA CLAUS!

CLOTHING SHOP IN MYRA, C. 320 AD

DO I REALLY NEED TO TRY THIS ON?

THIS IS MY GIFT TO YOU, NOW THAT YOU'RE A BISHOP. I WANT TO SEE YOU WEAR IT.

IT IS SAID THAT SANTA CLAUS' RED OUTFIT WAS INSPIRED BY THE RED VESTMENT THAT BISHOPS USED TO WEAR ON NICHOLAS' FEAST DAY (DECEMBER 6) WHEN THEY GAVE GIFTS TO THE POOR.

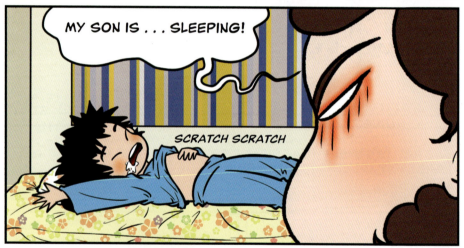

MY SON IS . . . SLEEPING!

SCRATCH SCRATCH

WAKE UP!

OPEN YOUR EYES!

OPEN BOTH OF YOUR EYES!

HOW MUCH OF THE STORY DID YOU HEAR?

I QUIT!

FROM NOW ON, YOU'RE ON YOUR OWN! YOU WILL COOK, DO LAUNDRY, AND STUDY ALL BY YOURSELF!

THIS IS THE WORST CRISIS OF MY LIFE! I NEED TO FIND A WAY OUT OF THIS!

FROM CRISIS MODE TO . . .
SURVIVAL MODE!

MOOOOOOOM

MOM, I WANT TO HEAR THE STORY.

REALLY?

YES! I REALLY WANT TO HEAR IT!

WHEW. I WILL NOT FALL ASLEEP THIS TIME. "SURVIVAL MODE" IS DIFFICULT.

SO, BEFORE THE STARVING BOY REACHED ONE HUNDRED, NICHOLAS TRADED CLOTHES WITH HIM. AND THEN . . .

SAINT NICHOLAS GAVE ALL HE HAD TO FOLLOW
JESUS AND SERVE HIM IN THE POOR. IN DOING SO,
HE BECAME AN INSTRUMENT OF GOD'S LIGHT AND
HOPE TO THE SUFFERING AND THE WEAK.

WE MUST LEARN TO IMITATE SAINT NICHOLAS' LOVE
AND GENEROSITY—ESPECIALLY AS WE CELEBRATE
THE BIRTH OF JESUS AT CHRISTMAS, WHICH IS
GOD'S GREATEST GIFT OF LOVE.

THE END